Dinosaurs Lived Here

written by Rona Putterman
illustrated by Tom Leonard

McGraw-Hill
School Division

New York   Farmington

D0189382

Dinosaurs first walked the Earth more than 220 million years ago. Back then, Earth looked very different from the way it looks today.

The World 240 Million Years Ago

The World 150 Million Years Ago

The World Today

Most scientists think that there was just one big continent, which they call Pangaea. The big continent slowly moved and finally broke into several pieces.

3

The first dinosaurs appeared in a time we call the Triassic Period. This period lasted from 245 to 208 million years ago. At that time the Earth was one big continent. Much of Pangaea was like a desert. It was hot and dry. Mountain peaks had only begun to form.

Many bones of early dinosaurs have been found in South Africa. One dinosaur found there is Lesothosaurus. Its name means "Lizard from Lesotho."

This small dinosaur lived more than 200 million years ago. It was only three feet long and ate plants.

Another dinosaur that lived in the same area was Massospondylus. This dinosaur was about 20 feet long and had a long neck. Scientists think it was one of the first plant-eating dinosaurs.

Time flowed along. Next came the Jurassic Period. This lasted until 146 million years ago. At the beginning of this period, there was still just one big continent. Earth was still hot and dry. But new types of trees and plants began to grow.

United States

New England

In the early part of this period, dinosaurs roamed what is now the East Coast of the United States. Fossils of Anchisaurus have been found in Massachusetts and Connecticut. This small dinosaur was between six and eight feet long. It weighed about 60 pounds. Scientists think it ate both meat and plants.

At the end of the Jurassic Period, the big
continent began to drift apart. Earth became
cooler and wetter. Shallow seas covered large
parts of the land. Much of the desert was
traded for thick, green forests.

At this time, many dinosaurs roamed what is now England. One was Dacentrurus. This spiked, plant-eating dinosaur was 15 feet long. It weighed about 1,500 pounds. Megalosaurus was another, more ferocious dinosaur that lived in the same area. Its name means "great lizard." This dinosaur was 10 feet tall, 30 feet long, and weighed more than 2,000 pounds.

In the Cretaceous Period, the continents moved even farther apart. By the end of this time, the shapes of the continents looked a lot like they do today. Flowering plants developed, and trees grew into thick, dark forests. We would be able to tell what some of these plants were if we saw them.

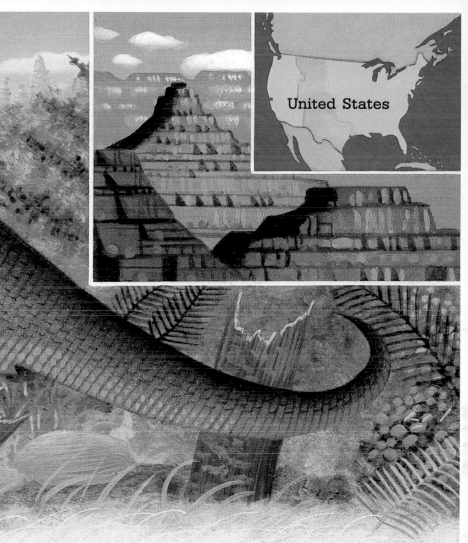

United States

The western United States is a great place to dig up dinosaur fossils from this time. Many have been found in pits, canyons, and valleys. Some of the dinosaurs that lived in this area were the three-horned Triceratops, duck-billed Maiasaura, and Tyrannosaurus Rex.

The T. rex is known as the king of all dinosaurs. Its name means "Tyrant Lizard King." Its fossils have been found in many western states, such as Texas, Montana, Utah, and Wyoming.

The Gobi Desert in Mongolia is a treasure chest for fossil hunters. The grains of hot, dry sand have preserved dinosaur bones for millions of years. Scientists have studied these bones and have learned a lot about dinosaurs. In 1924, they found the bones of an Oviraptor on top of a nest. The nest held a handful of eggs.

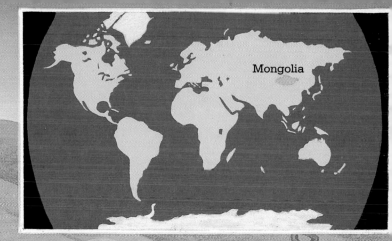
Mongolia

At first, scientists thought the Oviraptor had been eating the eggs. Recently scientists figured out that dinosaurs took care of their young.

One of the fiercest of all dinosaurs lived in the Gobi Desert. It was called Velociraptor. That means "quick hunter." This dinosaur had a big, sharp claw on each foot. These claws helped it quickly kill its prey.

For years, Antarctica was the only continent where no dinosaur fossils had been found. That changed in 1991. That's when scientists found the bones of a new type of dinosaur there. They named the dinosaur Cryolophosaurus. That means "frozen crested lizard."

Antarctica

This big dinosaur was a meat-eater. It had a high, narrow skull. The skull had a bony crest on top.

Dinosaur fossils are hard to find in Antarctica because they lie below the ice. But the continent wasn't always so cold. When it was part of Pangaea it was warm and mild.

At the end of the Cretaceous Period, all the
dinosaurs on Earth died out. No one knows how
this happened. Some scientists think an asteroid
smashed into Earth. Others think a huge volcanic
eruption killed the dinosaurs. We may never know
the real cause. But dinosaurs have been gone for
65 million years. All that is left are bones and
fossils. They tell the story of another time.

Story Questions and Activity

1. How long ago did the dinosaurs live?

2. Why do you think Massospondylus had such a long neck?

3. Why do you think scientists have found more fossils in the western United States than they have in Antarctica?

4. What is the main idea of the book?

5. What do you think Elizabeth's reaction might have been if she had found a dinosaur fossil on the beach?

Everything Changes!

Ask an older family member or neighbor how your hometown has changed over the years. What has remained the same? Write a paragraph describing what has stayed the same and what has changed. Tell what brought about the changes.

McGRAW-HILL READING

McGraw-Hill School Division

A Division of The McGraw·Hill Companies

ISBN 0-02-185170-0

99701

9 780021 851706

3·Bk·1·U·2

P7-EFP-364

Till a **letter** from Chloe arrived saying,
"Please, **please**, come over to play."

Polly ran all the way—she'd **missed** Chloe so much!
Chloe said, "We have **plenty to do**.

"Look at the toys and the games we can **share**,
they'll be twice as much **fun** now we're **two!**"

So Polly was **happy**, at very long last,
which was, after all, only fair.

Princesses have plenty, but never have fun
till they realize they do **love to share**.

Next Steps

- Ask your child what they know about princesses. Do they know where they live, what they look like, or what they wear?

- Talk about the different types of toys that your child has recently seen or played with.

- Ask your child why they think Polly kept all her toys to herself and why she did not allow anyone to come near any of them. Talk about how Polly might feel if she continued to think and behave this way about her toys.

- Can your child remember the name of Polly's friend? Discuss what her friend (Chloe) did when she arrived at Polly's house. Ask your child how Chloe felt about sharing things. How does this compare to how Polly felt about sharing? Does your child have any ideas of why these two girls might feel differently?

- Why does your child think Polly felt lonely and sad?

- Talk about what eventually made Polly feel happy. Can your child describe the picture on the last page? Make sure your child understands that sharing their toys with their friends can be more fun than playing alone.

- After reading the story together, ask your child how they feel when they play alone and how they feel when they play with their friends. Who does your child like to share their toys with?

Consultant: Cecilia A. Essau
Editor: Alexandra Koken
Designer: Andrew Crowson

Copyright © QEB Publishing 2012

First published in the United States by
QEB Publishing, Inc.
3 Wrigley, Suite A
Irvine, CA 92618

www.qed-publishing.co.uk

All rights reserved. No part of this publication may be
reproduced, stored in a retrieval system, or transmitted
in any form or by any means, electronic, mechanical,
photocopying, recording, or otherwise, without the prior
permission of the publisher, nor be otherwise circulated
in any form of binding or cover other than that in which
it is published and without a similar condition being
imposed on the subsequent purchaser.

ISBN 978 1 60992 344 0

Printed in China

Library of Congress Cataloging-in-Publication Data

Knapman, Timothy.
 Princesses love to share! / by Timothy Knapman ; illustrated
by Jimothy Rovolio.
    p. cm. -- (Marvelous manners)
 Summary: Polly owns many wonderful things, but learns from
her friend Chloe that they are even better when shared.
 ISBN 978-1-60992-267-2 (hardcover, library bound)
 [1. Stories in rhyme. 2. Sharing--Fiction. 3. Princesses--Fiction.]
I. Rovolio, Jimothy, ill. II. Title.
 PZ8.3.K73Pri 2013
 [E]--dc23

2011051886